Galapagos Rules!
Postcards from Poppies

Would you like for your child to make a book visit to the Galapagos Islands? These are some of the most pristine places left and will remain so as long as they are protected. Few children will have the opportunity to see the biodiversity one finds in these islands today. Travel with them as Poppies takes them through the islands in the book, *Galapagos Rules! Postcards from Poppies,* to learn the rules that protect all the diverse species on the islands. The book is comprised of stunning photos taken by the author.

Many of the descriptions of the animals given in the book were from notes taken from the Overseas Adventure Travel tour guide. However, these notes were checked for accuracy against the information provided on the Galapagos Conservancy website. I was able to gain more information from this website.

I would like to thank the Galapagos Conservancy via their website, https://www.galapagos.org/?utm_medium=email&utm_source=galapagos&utm_content=1&utm_campaign=AEKDENZZ&source=AEKDENZZ, for providing relevant information on the Galapagos species and the work they do to protect the environment and the animal life on the islands and seas around the islands. The Galapagos has been declared a National Park and World Heritage Site. Please visit their website to see the 14 actual rules for all visitors to the Park. I have listed some of the rules verbatim if in quotes within the story as I felt they apply to the specific photographs I took. Others I may have re-written.

Galapagos Rules!

Postcards from Poppies
Copyright 2019

Written by Lavelle Carlson
Photos by Lavelle Carlson

Enquiries should be addressed to:
info@slpstorytellers.com

First Edition

ISBN 13: 978-0-578-52391-0
ISBN 10: 0-578-52391-4

This book is dedicated to my husband, LeRoy (aka Poppies), and my two daughters, Liana and Lisa, who have given me five beautiful grandchildren, Taya, Niko, Emory, Rhodes, and Leni. It is also dedicated to all the beautiful children with whom I worked for many years as a speech/language pathologist.

Dear Explorer,

I flew into San Cristobal in the Galapagos Islands. The islands are a part of the country of Ecuador. The Galapagos is made up of many islands that were formed by volcanoes. The islands are a national park that tries to protect animals that are in danger of dying out. The Galapagos has rules to protect the environment and the animals. That is why we had to take a small ship from island to island. The park does not allow large cruise ships. As I travel to each island I will send you postcards of the animals. I am not sure where the post office is but I will get the cards in the mail as soon as I find one.

Love,
Poppies

GALAPAGOS

From:
Poppies
San Cristobal, Galapagos

To:

Young Explorer

Rule: "Travel only with tour operators and/or boats authorized to work in the protected areas of Galapagos."

Dear Explorer,

The small ship we took from San Cristobal does not travel to the shore of each island. I and the other visitors to the island climbed down a ladder on the small ship to small panga boats. We were taken to the shore of each island we visited. These small panga boats will ensure that less damage is done to the animals and the environment. There is less pollution from the smaller boats. There are also less people visiting the islands. This means there is less trash left to endanger the animals and sea life.

Love,
Poppies

P.S. I have not found a post office yet.

GALAPAGOS

From:
Poppies
San Cristobal Island

To:

Young Explorers

Dear Explorer,

This rule is to protect both you and the animals. The Galapagos does allow people to scuba dive in the waters around the islands, but only with a guide. You do not know what could be lurking in these trees. Watch for danger coming. Is that a shark? If you look close you can see the shark swimming below the water. It is good to follow the Galapagos rules to remain safe.

Love,
Poppies

I can see why there is not a post office here!

GALAPAGOS

From:
Poppies
Galapagos Islands

To:

Young Explorer

Rule: "Visitors to any protected areas within the Galapagos National Park must be accompanied by a naturalist guide authorized by the GNPD."

Dear Explorer,

Flash cameras can disturb the animals and birds. The sun provided good lighting so I was able to get some good pictures of my favorite bird, blue-footed booby. It is fun watching the boobies dive into the sea to catch sardines and herring for dinner. There are also red-footed boobies and Nasca boobies. How many times can you say "blue-footed booby"?

Love,
Poppies

I am looking for a post office to mail the cards.

GALAPAGOS

From:
Poppies
Isabela Island, Galapagos

To:

Young Explorer

Rule: "Flash photography is not permitted when taking photos of wildlife."

Dear Explorer,

These are Nasca boobies. They do not have blue feet like the blue-footed boobies. The Nasca boobies go out further into the sea than the blue-footed booby to hunt for their food. They build their nest on the ground like the blue-footed booby. It looks like these Nasca boobies are building a nest? Why do you think they are building a nest?

Love,
Poppies

I hope to find a post office soon so you can see these beautiful boobies.

GALAPAGOS

From:
Poppies
Galapagos Islands

To:

Young Explorer

Rule: "Maintain a distance of at least six feet (two meters) from wildlife to avoid disturbing them, even if they approach you."

Dear Explorer,

Do you see what I see? Look closely. I think I see one egg and one baby chick. Maybe the parents were building a nest for their family. Do you see a newborn chick and the egg? When the boobies fish for their food they quickly plunge into the sea. As they come up they catch their fish.

Love,
Poppies

I am still looking but cannot find a post office.

GALAPAGOS

From:
Poppies
Galapagos Islands

To:

Young Explorer

Dear Explorer,

Sally Lightfoot Crabs are the dancers in the Galapagos. Their legs are very nimble and fast. They have to be fast to survive and get away from the lava herons and lava lizards who like to eat them. Being nimble and fast also makes it easier to move among the rocks in search of their food. They are not picky eaters. They will eat almost anything (even bird poop). They use their sharp claws as spoons. One of these Sally Lightfoot crabs just washed in the sea. The other has been playing in the sand.

Maybe the post office will be at the next stop.

Love,
Poppies

From:
Poppies
Galapagos Islands

To:

Young Explorer

GALAPAGOS

Dear Explorer,

Charles Darwin was a famous scientist who studied all the finch birds on the different Galapagos islands. This helped us understand how they change in their environment; what they eat and how they live. The finches were all a little different on each island due to their different lifestyles and diet.

Love,
Poppies

Our tour guide said we will get to the post office soon.

From:
Poppies
Galapagos Islands

To:

Young Explorer

GALAPAGOS

Dear Explorer,

 Flamingos live in the saltwater lagoons. Young flamingos are born with grey plumage. As they get older the feathers turn a beautiful pink. The shrimp they eat has beta carotene that causes the flamingos' feathers to change to a pink color as they get older. Flamingos have beautiful long necks that can be curved into an "s" until it is time to reach down and catch a shrimp.

                    Love,
                    Poppies

I wonder if the flamingoes have seen many people looking for the post office.

GALAPAGOS

From:
Poppies
Galapagos Islands

To:

Young Explorer

Dear Explorer,

Yes, the Galapagos has pirates. It is not a man pirate. It is the frigate bird. They are often called a pirate or "man of war" because they like to swoop down and steal fish from the mouths of other birds. They are fast flyers and can easily catch up with other birds. They will catch fish and squid from the ocean.

Love,
Poppies

Still no post office!

GALAPAGOS

From:
Poppies
Floreana Island,
Galapagos

To:

Young Explorer

Dear Explorer,

This frigate mother flew out to sea and swooped down to catch the fish near the surface. She brought the food back to her young frigate bird. The young bird eats the small pieces out of its mom's mouth. Look how large the young frigate is. The mother is still feeding it.

Love,
Poppies

We were very quiet and did not ask where the post office is. We did not want to disturb the mother feeding the baby.

GALAPAGOS

From:
Poppies
Galapagos Islands

To:

Young Explorer

Dear Explorer,

Does this look like a wise owl to you or do you think he is saying, "Why are you taking a picture of me". I took the picture because he does look wise. There are two kinds of owls in the Galapagos, the barn owl and the short-eared owl. The barn owl's favorite food is rats and insects. They like to live in holes in trees but the short-eared owl lives under bushes.

Love,
Poppies

It is too bad the wise owl cannot talk to tell us where the post office is.

GALAPAGOS

From:
Poppies
Galapagos Islands

To:

Young Explorer

Dear Explorer,

Brown pelicans love to play in the waters around the Galapagos. This one is splashing so much it looks like it is taking a bubble bath. A pelican can be more than four feet long. But, the wings can be even wider than the pelican is long. The long wings help this pelican stir the water to make bubbles.

Love,
Poppies

This pelican is having too much fun to notice that we are taking pictures to mail at the post office when we find it.

GALAPAGOS

From:
Poppies
Galapagos Islands

To:

Young Explorer

Dear Explorer,

This pelican looks proud. It should be because it has learned a difficult way of feeding itself. When it goes out to sea to find fish to eat it scoops up more than two gallons of water in its beak. There are many small fish for the pelican's dinner. The pelican lets the water drain out and the pelican then eats the small fish that remain in its bill.

Love,
Poppies

GALAPAGOS

From:
Poppies
Galapagos Islands

To:

Young Explorer

Dear Explorer,

One would not expect to find penguins near the equator on the Galapagos Islands because penguins like the cold. So, they choose to live on one of the cooler islands, Fernandino, and maybe a couple of other cool islands. That way they can still live on the beautiful Galapagos and still will be a little cooler. They build their nests in caves on the shore. There are not many of these small penguins on the Galapagos so they are listed as endangered.

                    Love,
                    Poppies

Still no post office.

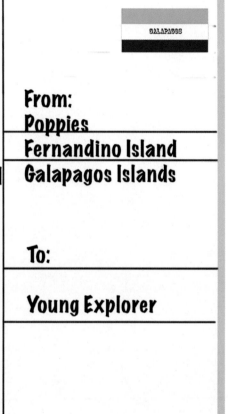

From:
Poppies
Fernandino Island
Galapagos Islands

To:

Young Explorer

Dear Explorer,

All iguanas are types of lizards but larger then the lizards you see where you live. This is a land iguana. He almost blends in with the lava rock he is sitting on. When it gets hot in the afternoon the iguanas will try to find a cactus shade or a tree. They will also eat from this same cactus that they sleep under in the afternoon. They dig burrows where they can sleep at night. It is cooler in the burrows.

Love,
Poppies

I hope I can find the post office so you can see these exciting animals!

GALAPAGOS

From:
Poppies
Santa Cruz Island
Galapagos Islands

To:

Young Explorer

Dear Explorer,

There is a reason that the Galapagos Park has the rule that you do not feed the animals. They have their own food that is good for them. What people eat may harm them. The marine iguanas are different from the land iguanas. They are the only sea going lizards in the world. They get their food from the rocks in the sea. They like to eat the algae that grow on the rocks. The different types of algae are almost like plants but there are no roots or leaves.

Love,
Poppies

No post office here - maybe it is too close to the sea.

From:
Poppies
Santa Cruz Island
Galapagos Islands

To:

Young Explorer

GALAPAGOS

Rule: "It is your responsibility not to introduce food, animals, or plants into the Archipelago. Cooperate fully with all environmental inspection and quarantine officials during your visit."

Dear Explorer,

 This marine iguana is sitting on a rock in the sunshine to stay warm. It lives on the land but eats seaweed on the rocks near the shore. The marine iguanas are sometimes called Christmas iguanas because of their color. When they are young they are usually gray. As they get older their color often turns red.

Love,
Poppies

This marine iquana looks scary enough that I do not think I want to go past him to look for the post office.

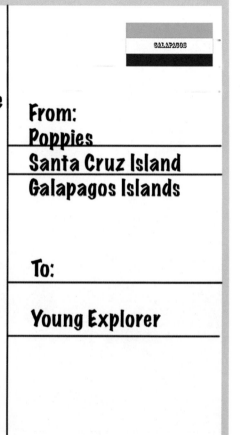

From:
Poppies
Santa Cruz Island
Galapagos Islands

To:

Young Explorer

Dear Explorer,

 The other way the marine iguanas are different from land iguanas is that they are very cold natured. They get sluggish when the temperature drops below 50 degrees. They have to come out of the sea onto the land to get warm. They also like to be close to one another. Are these friends keeping each other warm?

Love,
Poppies

Once I find that post office I will mail all the postcards.

GALAPAGOS

From:
Poppies
Santa Cruz Island
Galapagos Islands

To:

Young Explorer

Dear Explorer,

There are so many Marine iguanas. They like to travel together. I wonder where they are all going. Are they looking for a lunch of algae? Or, have they heard some small iguanas making fighting noises. We shall follow and see where they are going.

Love,
Poppies

Where is the post office?

GALAPAGOS

From:
Poppies
Isabela Island
Galapagos Islands

To:

Young Explorer

Dear Explorer,

It looks like the large group of marine iguanas knew something was going on. Are these iguanas really fighting or are they just playing a game?

Love,
Poppies

P. S. I still have not found the post office. I hope I find it soon. I really want you to enjoy these iguanas as much as I do.

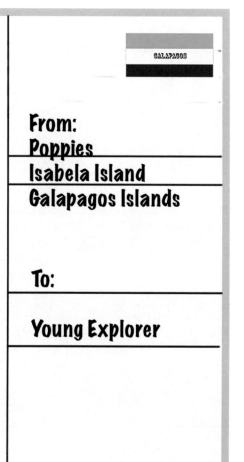

GALAPAGOS

From:
Poppies
Isabela Island
Galapagos Islands

To:

Young Explorer

Dear Explorer,

Remember the earlier rule that a tour guide
has to be with you for your safety. Well, the
sea lions are cute and it is tempting to get
close to them. But, the tour guide will tell
you to keep at a distance. The sea lions will
bite even though you are not their favorite
food, fish. They are the largest animals in
the Galapagos. I listened to the tour guide
and did not get close to pet them.

Love,
Poppies

I feel like I may be getting closer to a post
office.

From:
Poppies
Santa Cruz Island
Galapagos Islands

To:

Young Explorer

Rule: "A naturalist guide authorized by the GNPD must accompany visitors
to any protected areas within the Galapagos National Park."

Dear Explorer,

The Charles Darwin Research Station is the place where scientists work to save the giant Galápagos tortoises. They do this because the giant tortoises are in danger of dying off and becoming extinct.
There are several reasons many of them are dying and not reproducing. One of the greatest dangers is the plastic that people throw out. This plastic ends up in the sea and is then washed out into the Atlantic Ocean that surrounds the Galapagos Islands. The turtles swallow or get caught in it. That is why people in many countries are using less plastic.

Love,
Poppies

We are getting closer to the post office.

GALAPAGOS

From:
Poppies
Santa Cruz Island
Galapagos Islands

To:

Young Explorer

Rule: "Pack out all trash and dispose of or recycle it in the populated areas or on your tour boat."

Dear Explorer,

The Charles Darwin Research Station is the place where scientists work to save the giant Galápagos tortoises. They do this because the giant tortoises are in danger of dying off and becoming extinct.
There are several reasons many of them are dying and not reproducing. One of the greatest dangers is the plastic that people throw out. This plastic ends up in the sea and is then washed out into the Atlantic Ocean that surrounds the Galapagos Islands. The turtles swallow or get caught in it. That is why people in many countries are using less plastic.
                    Love,
                    Poppies
We are getting closer to the post office.

GALAPAGOS

From:
Poppies
Santa Cruz Island
Galapagos Islands

To:

Young Explorer

"Whatever happens to this single animal, let him always remind us that the fate of all living things on Earth is in human hands."

This inscription at Galapagos National Park is in honor of the most famous tortoise in the world, Lonesome George.

Dear Explorer,

Is this a turtle or tortoise. There are a couple of ways to tell the difference between a turtle and a tortoise? Turtles live mainly in or near water but come to land to lay eggs. See the turtle tracks in the sand. Their legs are more like flippers for swimming. Tortoises live only on land and cannot swim. Their legs are stubby. Tortoises are also bigger.

See the turtle tracks in the sand. The turtles have come to shore to lay their eggs. I was careful to watch for turtle eggs so I would not step on one.

Love,
Poppies

Where is the post office? It's time to go home.

GALAPAGOS

From:
Poppies
Santa Cruz Island
Galapagos Islands

To:

Young Explorer

Rule: Do not pick up and take shells, animal parts or other native mementos.

Dear Explorer,

I finally found the post office. It was not really a post office but just a mailbox on Floreana Island. It was put up in the 1700's when sailors came on ships to explore the Galapagos. The sailors needed a way to send mail to their families far away.
A sailor put up a barrel where letters could be placed until a ship came. When the ship came it took the letters back to their families in their home country. The ship did not come often so it was a long time for their families to get their mail and a long time for their families to send them mail. The mailbox is still used by visitors to the islands today. I am putting my postcards in this mailbox for you.

Love,
Poppies

GALAPAGOS

From:
Poppies
Floreana Island
Galapagos Islands

To:

Young Explorer

Poppies mailing postcards from
Floreana, Galapagos Islands

More books for early childhood and speech/language and fun:

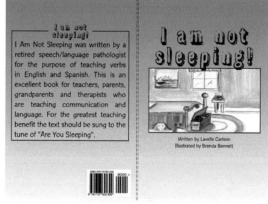

Made in the USA
Columbia, SC
03 March 2020